MIDDLE
PASSAGES

Also by Kamau Brathwaite

P O E T R Y

The Arrivants: A New World Trilogy (Oxford University Press, 1973),
    comprising:
  Rights of Passage (OUP, 1967)
  Masks (OUP, 1968)
  Islands (OUP, 1969)
The second (Bajan) trilogy comprising:
  Mother Poem (OUP, 1977)
  Sun Poem (OUP, 1982)
  X/Self (OUP, 1987)
Other Exiles (OUP, 1975)
Days & Nights (Caldwell Press, Mona, Jamaica, 1975)
Black + Blues (Casa de las Americas, Havana, Cuba, 1976)
Soweto (Savacou, Mona, Jamaica, 1979)
Word Making Man (Savacou, Mona, Jamaica, 1979)
Third World Poems (Longman, 1983)
Jah Music (Savacou, Mona, Jamaica, 1986)
Sappho Sakyi's Meditations (Savacou, Mona, Jamaica, 1990)
Shar/Hurricane Poem (Savacou, Mona, Jamaica, 1990)
MiddlePassages (Bloodaxe Books, 1992)

P L A Y S

Four Plays for Primary Schools (Longman, 1964)
Odale's Choice (Evans, 1967)

O T H E R   B O O K S

The People Who Come 1-3 (Longman, 1968–72; new edition 1990–92)
Folk Culture of the Slaves in Jamaica (New Beacon, 1970)
The Development of Creole Society in Jamaica 1770–1820 (Clarendon Press, 1971)
Contradictory Omens (Savacou, Mona, Jamaica, 1974)
Our Ancestral Heritage (Carifesta, Kingston, Jamaica, 1976)
Wars of Respect (API, Kingston, Jamaica, 1977)
Jamaica Poetry: A Checklist 1686–1978 (Jamaica Library Service, Kingston, 1979)
Barbados Poetry: A Checklist (Savacou, Jamaica, 1979)
The Colonial Encounter: Language (University of Mysore, India, 1984)
*History of the Voice: The Development of Nation Language in Anglophone
    Caribbean Poetry* (New Beacon, 1984)
Roots: essays in Caribbean literature (Casa de las Americas, Havana, Cuba,
    1986; new edition, University of Michigan Press, Ann Arbor, 1993)
The Zea Mexican Diary (University of Wisconsin Press, Madison, 1993)

KAMAU BRATHWAITE

MIDDLE PASSAGES

A NEW DIRECTIONS BOOK

Acknowledgements

Acknowledgements are due to the publishers of the following books and pamphlets in which earlier versions of some of these poems first appeared: *Rights of Passage* (Oxford University Press, 1967), for 'Colombe'; *Islands* (OUP, 1969), for 'Leopard'; *Word Making Man* and *Soweto* (both Savacou, Mona, Jamaica, 1979) for the poems of those titles; *Sun Poem* (OUP, 1982), for 'Noom'; *Third World Poems* (Longman, 1983), for 'The Visibility Trigger', 'How Europe underdeveloped Africa' and 'Irae'; *X/Self* (OUP, 1987), for 'Veridian', 'Sahel', 'Letter Sycorax' and 'Irae'. 'Stone' was first published in Britain in the magazine *Artrage* and in the anthology *Hinterland: Caribbean Poetry from the West Indies & Britain* (Bloodaxe Books, 1989), and in the Caribbean in *Jah Music* (Savacou, Mona, Jamaica, 1986), as was 'Flute(s)'.
Manufactured in the United States of America.
New Directions Books are printed on acid-free paper.
MiddlePassages was published in 1992 by Bloodaxe Books, Newcastle Upon Tyne,·England. The New Directions edition incorporates the author's revisions.
First published as New Directions Paperbook 776 in 1993.
Text based on "Sycorax video style" being developed by Kamau Brathwaite.

Library of Congress Cataloging in Publication Data

Brathwaite, Kamau. 1930–
    Middle passages / Kamau Brathwaite.
      p. cm.
    ISBN 0–8112–1232–7
    I. Title. II. Title: MiddlePassages.
  PR9230.9.B68M54   1993
811—dc20   93–17249
                                                          CIP
                                                          Rev.

New Directions Books are published for James Laughlin
by New Directions Publishing Corporation,
80 Eighth Avenue, New York 10011

for Gordon Rohlehr

WORD MAKING MAN

poem for Nicolás Guillén in Xaymaca

S ir,

not in 'Sir'
but *compañero*
as you wd prefer it in *hispañol*

i have not yet been to cuba
& do not know the language of yr *oradores*
& as you said

'some of us are champions
from the provinces, others
lo son olímpicos.' & some of us
are nothing — you will forgive me if i quote you again —
'not even *oradores'*

but i know that we are watching in a long circle for the dawn
& that the ruling class does not wait at bus stops
& i know that we are watching in a long circle for the fire
& that our *compradores* do not ladle soup out of the yabba

in camagüey
            ave maría
                  católica

silversmith turned silverfish. your father
in the leaves of the spanish classics. metallic needlework
in a tropic of paper. turblethumb thimbleprint journalist
who divined the omens of martí

when he was shot — *fusilamiento*
you became a snake
circling circling circling renewing yr cycle of certainty

& you awoke to sleepy horses
sleepy snocone vendors
to hazy drunkards staggering to their homes

you tripped you cried you stumbled
on the dreams of those far-off days:

nicotine lópez, yr pharmacist & friend
the town clerk cores and the cop who died his name like caanan
what's his name?

& serafin toledo. blacksmith steel-lightning tailor
'& the school desk w/ the pen-knife scars
beneath a sky of fireflies & stars'

& we all learn
guitarra
we all learn

mayombe-bombe-mayombé
mayombe-bombe-mayombé

that one does not kill a brother
that one does not kill a brother
that one does not kill a brother

& look how   *sensemayá*   he is dead!

■

Now we rock-steady safely in the *orisha* of our dreams
& yr name has become the *sunsum* of our ancestors

to the pale salons of the *lippi* song you brought the *son*
w/ the broad boa of the *conquistadore* violin you bent the tree

4

jack johnson   kid chocolate   muhammad ali
them jazzers w/ cow-punches in their smiles

the stylish patent-leather shoes, the creaking
downstairs down the stares from broadway stretching

out 'its snout, its moist enormous mout
to lick & glut upon our canefields' vital blood'

black little rock. the mau mau. emmett till
guevara & the beaten skulls of biko & lumumba

you have whispered it all. you have uttered it all
coriolan of blood. plankton of melt & plangent syllables

sunrise *lucumi* sparkle

against yr teeth of joy
sus dientes de júbilo

amerika laughs
west indies west indies west indies ltd

■

but suddenly in the night of possibility
it turns to the wall in its creaking bed of dollars

west indies west indies west indies unlimited

& yr voice rises like the moon
above the day of pigs . above the choruses of

who is it? who is it not?
the negro

who is it? who is it not?
my hunger

who is it? who is it not?
i & i talkin to ya

& the sea between us yields its secrets
silver into pellables into sheets of sound
that bear our pain & spume & salt & coltrane

saying
xangô

'no
not no
not bad
not bad, not velly bad'

but

yes
sí yes
bien
sí well
sí velly well

so that we learn w/you the pleasure
of walking w/our roots across the country

owners herein of all there is to see
owners herein of what we must believe
of what our hands encompass as we dream

so that together we say wind
& understand its history of ghosts
together we say fire

& again there is a future in those sparks
together, comrade, friend
we say this is our land & know at last at last it is our home

now mine forever & so yours, *amigo*
ours
'w/ the vast splendour of the sunshine & the sunflower & the stars'

Colombe

Columbus from his after-
deck watched stars, absorbed in water,
melt in liquid amber drifting

through my summer air
Now with morning shadows lifting
beaches stretched before him cold & clear

Birds circled flapping flag & mizzen
mast. birds harshly hawking. without fear
Discovery he sailed for. was so near

Columbus from his after-
deck watched heights he hoped for
rocks he dreamed. rise solid from my simple water

Parrots screamed. Soon he would touch
our land. his charted mind's desire
The blue sky blessed the morning with its fire

But did his vision
fashion as he watched the shore
the slaughter that his soldiers

furthered here? Pike
point & musket butt
hot splintered courage. bones

cracked with bullet shot
tipped black boot in my belly. the
whips uncurled desire?

olumbus from his after-
deck saw bearded fig trees. yellow pouis
blazed like pollen & thin

waterfalls suspended in the green
as his eyes climbed towards the highest ridges
where our farms were hidden

Now he was sure
he heard soft voices mocking in the leaves
What did this journey mean. this

new world mean. dis
covery? or a return to terrors
he had sailed from. known before?

I watched him pause

Then he was splashing silence
Crabs snapped their claws
and scattered as he walked towards our shore

Damballa

Νοομ

When the sun shine on the polyps

they become shells
and before the fish had rippled scales over their spongy flesh
the skulls had become hills

and the hills grew green as the grass took root & flourished

■

a ship came, seeking harbour, fleeing from torture & swords
and a sugarcane sprouted
it grew taller than the crab grass & the nettle
it grew taller
and its owners shouted for their women to behold this sibilant
miracle

they brought knives & cutlasses & bill hooks & baskets
hoping to reap rich harvest
but the sun was too hot & their waxen flesh
melted like candles of fetish or faith within their wooden churchicles

they saw their prophets recede like hope like mirage
and they worried about their courage
and that the brown islam might become a green desert of fields
some deserted the choral
and fled to more flattering glacial man/scapes
fishing in nova scotia sharpshooting engines along the navajo trail
refrigerating their meals

■

the ones who remained grew black in the face
and their grey folded thoughts tuned to africa

there are tribes there of scarcecrows
hunters of heads who ate humane bones
crink skull & cavicle

big buttock women who preferred to mate with baboons
orangoutangs who ate oranges like well trained children in our zoos

they knew maize: yes: and yam & cassava
could fashion aztecs of beads to cover their naked zon.
goes were skilful with muddum & clayfish

they used wood well & pounded their grain into their own
fashioned mortars. were mortal
and worshipped the devil like

henry viii like leo x like francis i like pope joan
of arc like baptists like jesuit priests like ni
collo machiavelli like the niggers they were

they caught alligators to make tooth
charms against the spine
ache. against spear thrust & man

drake
but they didn't know bulls barcelona or bullets
they couldn't claim comfort of clergy

fine

(origins of slavery)

we'll let columbus deal with this matter. he has three ships
that will import them. the *nina*
will take six hundred from senegal
the *pinta* will take on five thousand — the boatswain will make them

hold at the côte d'ivoire & the gambia
and the admiral's caravel flagship will sail on down the coast
crossing the terrors of equatorial miasma
until it reaches the tong of the congo

it will throttle its anchor down into the cold muddy morn
ing water of the man
grove swamps & manacles and it will wait
sooner or later a man with a fan or a lion or loin cloth. bare

foot or in pal. anquin will rise to the bait
mumbled by drummers & several fearful attendants
do not run
abate them with bullet or bribe

better bribe if you can
preserve the bullets for naygars
and bring back a hundred thousand
this isn't no joke

remember what happened to raleigh & drake

above all, love
ignore their songs their manimal membranes resounding with
the sounds of their godderel
and don't try to learn their langridge. teach them spanglish

preach them rum

ignore too the customs of their courts. the loaves
of their bread do not float on the water. what you break
you must eat. therefore

do not seduce the headman's wife but his cook
what he loves he will flart. look
to it. your cock might depend upon

it

and their are ceritain noblemen. their priests you might call
them. who talk too much & mutter & make zodiac
signs & have. you will find. a great deal of influence
among the warriors & older women

stick knives through their tongues
and when the ship sails for the fair winds of the azores
strangle them drunk & dunk them overboard
the dolphins will weep while the sharks rip their watery groves

Duke

Playing Piano at 70

for
Tom Dent
+
Anne Walmsley at 60

■

The old man's hands are alligator
skins
and swimming easily like these
along the harp stringed keyboard
where he will make
of
Solitude
a silver thing
as if great age like his
could play that tune along
these cracks that flow
between their swing
without a scratch of thistle
sound
& whistle down the rhythm all night long

&

what a way to love you madly madly madly
with the wisdom of so many
all night carioca smokes
& dish & clutter knife & clatter up the bad bo
didley barrios

■

my Uncle Bigard

fix.
ing in the piss stained

RESTROOMS

mood & oboe
indigo

■

wet glass
of

SUPER
NOVA HEADLIGHTS

O

Bessie
Bessie
Bessie Smith
the empress of our shattered blues

you
smiling up front in the coach
avery morning
after the thousand & one one night stands

Watts
St Louis
Selma Alabama
Chicago
Montgomery Bus Boycott
Cairo
where they most nearly kill you

Sphinx
Pharaoh
Memphis Tennessee
where they did where they did
where they finally did

but
the happy-go-lucky-locals
shout. in
out

run Jesse **run**

Jesse **run** Jesse

run

call yo out.
cast. low
down
you cain't make
it
you're nothin. you're from no.
body
3rd class servant class got-no-class underclass

it is not a question my friends
about a telephone call
of who tango with who
of who shit. in with who in the shithouse

is a matter of hope of keep hope alive of the right to continue the
dream
about our rightful place at the table

&

the curtain psyching up
& the lights swimming down into such sweet thunder of silence

& each time each time is like that creak before birth
Jimmy Hamilton's wood-lip-like carolina clarinet
leading us out of the silence

■

Afternoon of a saxophone
Caravan
Perdido
Cottontail
Satin Doll
Sophisticated Lady
Transblucency
the creo
Creole Love Call
Creole Dawn

&

let me hear it one more time
for

IVIE
ANDERSONNNG

&

DC
in summer

hot almost too simmer to sip . sop . sit out on the stoep
w/ old men from the neighbourhood .

cymbell children

cries rising like these northern egrets
above the railway tracks
where Sonny Greer come walk.
ing down the sidewalk clickin sticks

■

The old man plays the tune
with ancient hands of jungle tints & mumble floods
of vamp piano at the Cotton Club

New Orleans woman drum
Gonsalves
Rabbit
Harry Carney
Cootie
Nanton
Woodyard
Blanton
Cat

the
doo-doo doo-doo wah
of
Harlem Air-Shaft

warm & deep where I am born upon the sidewalk
on the corner . in the precinct with no father to my name . no
name
but what my grandma gave me
our mother dragging us across
the midnight city looking for a place
to sleep
at least to heat her box of broken innings in . taking two jobs
like twins
so she could reap us chicken bones
to keep our hopes alive

not one a we   she always say *too poor*
to hear a pride
a Ko-Ko trombone lion roar

■

the old man's hands are striding through
the keyboard sidewalks alleyways & ages

from
Shakka spear and guinea Bird

to
Caribbean stilt dance
vèvè
masquerade

&
Buddy Bolden's golden Strayhorn horn across the misty
goombay levee dawn
that no sleak jazzhouse perfume scent can cheapen

27

■

his hands are playing every Tricky Nanton book in town
black black Black Bottom Stomp
diminuendo honey beige & hallelujah brown

■

& look
the old man's alligator hands are young

Flute (♪)

for
Dream Chad & Pamela Mordecai

is when the bamboo from its clip of yellow groan & wrestle
begins to glow & the wind learns the shape of its fire
and my fingers following the termites drill
drip into their hollows of silence . shatters of echoes of tone

that my eyes close all along the walling . all along the branches .
all along the world
and that that creak of spirits walking these graves of sunlight
spiders over the water . cobwebs crawling in whispers
over the stampen green

find

from a distance so cool it is a hill in haze
it is a fish of shadow along the sandy bottom
it is a butterfly alight the blossom
and that the wind is following my footsteps

all along the rustle all along the echoes all along the world
and that that stutter I had heard in some dark summer freedom
startles & slips from fingertip to fingerstop
into the float of the morning into the throat of its sound

it is a baby mouth but softer than the suck it makes
it is a hammock sleeping in the shadow
it is a hammer shining in the shade

it is the kite ascending chord & croon & screamers
it is the cloud that curls to hide the eagle
it is the ripple of the stream from bamboo

it is the ripple of the stream from blue
it is the gurgle pigeon dream the ground doves coo
it is the sun approaching midday listening its splendour

it is your voice alight with echo . with the bright of sound

Veridian

for Grandee Nanny & the Chankofi people of Palmares

High up in this littered world of rock. stone

yucca bush bamboo trash narrow
defiles where there are no sweet painted trees

wind we know always sharp slant sleet howl but warm
as yr lips & gentle as a mother w/her baby cheek
to cheek misty mornings high noons spectacular sunsets

at the bottom of this high world above it all we draw
the lion picket our stand & make our testament
boy girl woman warrior elder statesman gunsmith technician food
engineer shamir shama shaman we are all gathered here

guerrilla camouflage flack. jacket
ambuscade thorny stockade. we smell
our cooking & our evening
smoke. the little ones collect
the firewood. i feel

the fire flickering my back. even from five hundred paces
in this hammock
everything looks inward to this centre
we are not taken lightly in our cups
or in our sleeping bags . shocked by surprise
the sentinels along our lifeline ledge of echoes

come down the hill at sunrise w/eyes that read the dark
m16s that are not

                                                        crutches
             though we might hold them o so casual against our sides

we have been visited by goddesses & loan sharks from across the
                                water. from lomé & from abidjan

     we make the same blue cloth they make we mix our mortar
similar. our tongues are always rough & bark & slark like theirs

                                             from the same bissi

     when children suck their fingers after we have weaned them
                        from their mother's best breast suppligen
we paint the same green aloes on their thin slimy biscuit finger

tips & wonder if they ever going to learn there's mullet shrimp
  & janga in the rivers & ganja in the harvest valley villages
               & gungo peas behind the pissitoires

     & yet today the hawks on their warm rising roundabouts
               look like dark sorrows . for the portuguese
               have beaten us at last at their own game

          surrounded us . camped hard all year against us .
revved rockets up into the very kidneys of our cooking pots
beguiled the younger female fauns w/foolish fans & beauty

contestants . have taught them shave their midden hair & brave.
          ly bare a buonorott' bikini sheer & mare & tender
loin & how i gonna bring you in a early morning breakfast plate

          tourists let inroads by the sweeper at the market gate
               rush in & shoot us w/their latest nikon leicas
& many of our men are lured away to work at chipping ice in sin.

                                                        cinnati

cutting the canal at christopher
columbus place in pan
ama to scraping braille off battleships'

blind grey green under.
water bellies: vieques porto bello choc guantanamo bahia O
black cat nanny nanahemm. do not desert us now don't let the

harm.

attan come ridin high in here sieve sand through
intestine & wickerwork cassava matapee
prick grit through fish its open golden underwater eye
dry all the all-day-long sky water up

so that the hillslides come out yellow yellow poui &
catch fire in the morning grow
so that the leaves of callaloo will quail
so that we cannot plant olodumare yam even in this high tinder

season

i remember the dogs here

runagate
runagate
runagate

harsp breath bleak teeth the tongue that sees us all

runagate
runagate
runagate

i remember the red ride raider high up on his horse
spur like an eagle horn
hibiscus spurting from the rearing flanks
drumming upon my heed at noon
my blind eye thorn out looted looted looted

runagate
runagate
runagate

i remember the chain
& the chain-gang sweat
& the gong-gongs of disaster

runagate
runagate
runagate

did i escape the sharp dark crystal graze of the square
foot dog for this

the shooken sugar factory furnace door of the plantation blaze
for this

runagate
runagate
runagate

look how our villages are grown up tall
into this strangled city
tales of another leader lost
solares . bolivare . palanquin

washed away w/time & frogs & river & the mud & accompong

The Visibility Trigger

for
Kwame Nkrumah
& the leaders of the Third World

■

and so they came up over the reefs

up the creeks & rivers
oar prong put-put
hack tramp silence

and i was dreaming near morning

i offered you a kola nut
your fingers huge & smooth & red
and you took it your dress makola blue

and you broke it into gunfire

■

the metal was hot & jagged
it was as if the master of bronze
had poured anger into his cauldron

and let it spit spit sputter
and it was black spark green in my face
it was as if a maggot had slapped me in the belly

and i had gone soft like the kneed of my wife's bread

i could hear salt leaking out of the black hole of kaneshie
i could hear grass growing around the edges of the green lake
i could hear stalactites ringing in my cave of vision

bats batting my eyes shut
their own eyes howling like owls in the dead dark

and they marched into the village
and our five unready virginal elders met them

bowl calabash oil carafe of fire silence

and unprepared & venerable I was dreaming mighty wind in trees
our circles talismans round hut round village cooking pots

the world was round & we the spices in it
time wheeled around our memories like stars

yam cassava groundnut sweetpea bush
and then it was yams again

birth child hunter warrior
and the breath

that is no more

43

which is birth which is child which is hunter which is warrior
which is breath

that is no more

■

and they brought sticks rods roads bullets straight objects
birth was not breath

but gaping wound

hunter was not animal
but market sale

warrior was child
that is no more

and i beheld the cotton tree
guardian of graves rise upward from its monument of
grass

■

crying aloud in its vertical hull
calling for crashes of branches vibrations of leaves

there was a lull of silver

■

and then the great grandfather gnashing upwards from its teeth
of roots. split down its central thunder

the stripped violated wood crying aloud its murder. the leaves'
frontier signals alive with lamentations

and our great odoum
triggered at last by the ancestors into your visibility

crashed
into history

How Europe underdeveloped Africa

for Mexican & Walter Rodney

to be blown into fragments. your flesh
like the islands that you loved
like the seawall that you wished to heal

bringing equal rights & justice to the brothers
a fearless cumfa mashramani to the sisters whispering their
free/zon
that grandee nanny's histories be listened to with all their ancient

flèches of respect

until they are the steps up the poor of the church
up from the floor of the hill/slide
until they become the roar of the nation

that fathers would at last settle into what they own
axe adze if not oil well. torch
light of mackenzie

that those who have all these generations
bitten us bare to the bone
gnawing our knuckles to their stone

price fix price rise rachman & rat/chet squeeze
how bread is hard to buy how rice is scarcer than the
muddy water where it rides

how bonny baby bellies grow doom-laden dungeon grounded down
to groaning in their hunger
grow wailer voiced & red eyed in their anger

that knocks against their xylophones of prison ribs
that how we cannot give our wives or sleephearts or our children
or our children's children a sweetend trip to kenya. watch

maasai signal from their saffron shadow
the waterbuck & giraffe wheel round wrecked manyatta
while little blonder kinter

who don't really give a fart
for whom this is the one more yard
a flim. for whom this is the one/off start

to colon cortez cecil rhodes
for whom this is the one more road
to the soff-voiced thathi-headed waiter

aban. died out of his shit by his baas. at the nairobi airport hotel

but lets his face sulk into i soup
lets his hairshirt wrackle i sweat
cause i man am wearing the tam of his dream in i head

that these & those who fly still dread/er up the sky
vultures & hawks. eye
scarpering morgan the mi/ami mogol

those night beast a babylon who heiss us on sus

but that worse it is the blink
in iani own eye. the sun blott. ed out by
paper a cane fires vamp.

ires a ink wheels emp.
ires a status quo status quo status crows
that tell a blood tale toll/ing in the ghetto

till these small miss/demeanours as you call them
be
come a monstrous fetter on the land that will not let us breed

un. til every chupse in the face of good morning
be
come one more coil one more spring one more no

thing to sing/about
be
come the boulder rising in the bleed

the shoulder nourishing the gun
the headlines screaming of the skrawl across the wall
of surbiton of trenton town of sheraton hotel

dat POR CYAAAN TEK NO MOOR

& the babies & their mothers & their mothers & their
mothers mothers & their mothers mothers mothers mothers
sizzled forever in the semi-automatic catcalls of the orange heat

flare up of siren. howl of the scorch wind wail
through the rat-tat-rat-a-tat-tat
of the hool through the tap of your head. damp. stench. criall

the well of war flame drilling through your flesh

reduced to the time before green/bone
reduced to the time before ash/skull
reduced to the time before love/was born

in your arms
before dawn was torn from your pillow
in your arms

before the tumours were crumpled into paper bags
inside the star/broek market

in your arms

before the knife ran through the dark & locket steel
between the spine & kidney

in your arms
in your arms
in your arms

i prophesay

before you recognized the gorgon head inside the red eye
of the walkie talkie

■

to be blown into fragments. your death
like the islands that you loved
like the seawall that you wished to heal

bringing equal rights & justice to the bredren
that the children above all others would be like the sun.
rise

over the rupununi over the hazy morne de castries over kilimanjaro

any where or word where there is love there is the sky & its blue
free
where past means present struggle

towards vlissengens where it may some day end

distant like powis on the essequibo
drifting like miracles or dream
or like that lonely fishing engine slowly losing us its sound

but real like your wrist with its tick of blood around its man.
acles of bone
but real like the long marches the court steps of tryall

the sudden sodden night journeys up the pomeroon
holed up in a different safe house every morning & try
ing to guess from the heat of the hand.

shake if the stranger was stranger or cobra or friend
& the urgent steel of the kis.
kadee glittering its *qqurl* down the steepest bend in the breeze

& the leaves

ticking & learning to live with the smell of rum on the skull's
breath. his cigarette ash on the smudge of your fingers
his footsteps into your houses

& having to say it over & over & over again
with your soft ringing patience with your black.
lash of wit. though the edges must have been curling with pain

but the certainty clearer & clearer & clearer again

that it must be too simple to hit/too hurt
not to remember

that it must not become an easy slogan or target
too torn too defaced too devalued down in redemption market

that when men gather govern other manner
they should be honest in a world of hornets

that bleed into their heads like lice
corruption that cockroaches like a dirty kitchen sink

that politics should be like understanding of the floor.
boards of your house

swept clean each morning. built by hands that know
the wind & tide & language

from the loops within the ridges of the koker
to the rusty tinnin fences of your yard

so that each man on his cramped restless island
on backdam of his land in forest clearing by the broeken river
where berbice struggles against slushy ground

takes up his bed & walks

in the power & the reggae of his soul/stice
from the crippled brambled pathways of his vision
to the certain limpen knowledge of his nam

■

this is the message that the dreadren will deliver
groundation of the soul with drift of mustard seed

that when he spoke the world was fluter on his breeze
since it was natural to him like the water. like the way he listened

like the way he walked. one a dem ital brothers who had grace

for being all these things & careful of it too
& careless of it too
he was cut down plantation cane

because he dared to grow & growing/green
because he was that slender reed & there were machetes sharp
enough to hasten him & bleed

he was blown down

because his bridge from man to men
meant doom to prisons of a world we never made
meant wracking out the weeds that kill our yampe vine

■

& so the bomb
fragmenting islands like the land you loved

letting back darkness in

■

but there are stars that burn that murders do not kno·
soft diamonds behind the blown to bits

that trackers will not find that bombers will not see
that scavengers will never hide away

■

the caribbean bleeds near georgetown prison

■

a widow rushes out & hauls her children free

STONE

for Mikey Smith 1954–1983
stoned to death on Stony Hill, Kingston

When the stone fall that morning out of the johncrow sky

it was not dark at first . that opening on to the red sea humming
but something in my mouth like feathers . blue like bubbles
carrying signals & planets & the sliding curve of the
world like a water pic. ture in a raindrop when the pressure. drop

W hen the stone fall that morning out of the johncrow sky

i couldn't cry out because my mouth was full of beast & plunder
as if i was gnashing badwords among tombstones
as if that road up stony hill. round the bend by the church
yard . on the way to the post office . was a bad bad dream

& the dream was like a snarl of broken copper wire zig zagg.
ing its electric flashes up the hill & splitt. ing spark & flow.
ers high. er up the hill . past the white houses & the ogogs bark.
ing all teeth & fur. nace & my mother like she up . like she up.

like she up. side down up a tree like she was scream.
like she was scream. like she was scream. in no & no.
body i could hear could hear a word i say. in . even though
there were so many poems left & the tape was switched on &

runn. in & runn. in &
the green light was red & they was stannin up there &
evva. where in london & amsterdam & at unesco in paris &
in west berlin & clapp. in & clapp. in & clapp. in &

not a soul on stony hill to even say amen

■

& yet it was happenin happenin happenin

the fences begin to crack in i skull .
& there was a loud boodoooooooooooooooooooooooongs like
guns going off . them ole time magnums .

or like a fireworks a dreadlocks was on fire .
& the gaps where the river comin down
inna the drei gully where my teeth use to be smilin .
& i tuff gong tongue that use to press against them & parade

pronunciation . now unannounce & like a black wick in i head &
dead .
& it was like a heavy heavy riddim low down in i belly . bleedin dub
& there was like this heavy heavy black dog thump. in in i chest &

pump. in

murderrrrrrrrrrrrrrrrrrrrrrrrrrrrrrrrrrrrrrrrrrrrrrrrrrrrrrr

& i throat like dem tie. like dem tie. like dem tie a tight tie a.
round it. twist. in my name quick crick . quick crick .
& a nevva wear neck. tie yet .

& a hear when de big boot kick down i door . stump
in it foot pun a knot in de floor. board .
a window slam shat at de back a mi heart .

de itch & oooze & damp a de yaaad
in my silver tam. bourines closer & closer .
st joseph marching bands crash. in & closer . &

bom si. cai si. ca boom ship bell . bom si. cai si. ca boom ship bell

& a laughin more blood & spittin out
lawwwwwwwwwwwwwwwwwwwwwwwwwwwwwwwwwwwwwwwwwd

61

i two eye lock to the sun & the two sun starin back black
from de grass

& a bline to de butterfly fly. in

■

& it was like a wave on stony hill caught in a crust of sun.
light

■

& it was like a matchstick schooner into harbour muffled in the
silence of it wound

■

& it was like the blue of speace was filling up the heavens
wid its thunder

& it was like the wind was grow. in skin. the skin had hard hairs
harderin

■

it was like marcus garvey rising from his coin .
stepping towards his people crying dark

& every mighty word he trod. the ground fall dark & hole
be. hine him like it was a bloom x. ploding sound .

my ears was bleed. in sound

■

& i was quiet now because i had become that sound

the sun. light morning washed the choral limestone harsh
against the soft volcanic ash. i was

& i was slippin past me into water. & i was slippin past me
into root. i was

& i was
slippin past me into flower. & i was rippin upwards

into shoot. i was

& every politrician tongue in town was lash.
ing me with spit & cut. rass wit & ivy whip & wrinkle jumbimum

it was like warthog . grunt. in in the ground

& children running down the hill run right on through the splash
of pouis that my breathe. ing make when it was howl & red &

bubble

& sparrow twits pluck tic & tap. worm from the grass
as if i man did nevva have no face. as if i man did never in this

place

■

W hen the stone fall that morning out of the johncrow sky

i could not hold it brack or black it back or block it off or limp
away or roll it from me into memory or light or rock it steady
into night. be

cause it builds me now with leaf & spiderweb & soft & crunch &
like the pow.
derwhite & slip & grit inside your leather. boot &

fills my blood with deaf my bone with hobbledumb & echo.
less neglect neglect neglect neglect &

lawwwwwwwwwwwwwwwwwwwwwwwwwwwwwwwwwwwwww

■

i am the stone that kills me

The
Sahell
of
Donatello

Rome burns
& our slavery begins

in the alps
oven of europe

glacier of god
chad's opposite

industry was envisioned here in the indomitable glitter
it out proportions parthenon

the colosseum is not to be compared with it
nor dome nor london bridge bernini bronze nor donatello

marble

there is more wealth here than with the bankers of amsterdam
more power than in any boulder dam of heaven

volt crackle & electricity it has invented
buchenwald nagasaki & napalm

it is the frozen first atomic bomb
its factories blaze forth bergs & avalanches

its unships sail down rhine down rhône
down po down dan down tiber

to the black sea dead to the world to the red sea of isaias

without it the sahara would have been water
latvium carthage tunis would have been dolphin towns

genoa would have become a finchal of the esquimaux
columbus would have sailed south along the congo's rivers

but being immobil:e here
more permanent than pope or charlemagne

it has burnt rome
but preserved europe

as it rises

chad sinks

sa
hara wakes out slowly

the sly dry snake of the harm
attan. reaches into our wells into our smiles. in

to our cook
ing pot oil. in

to the water re.

flecting our walls in.

to our dry gully eyes

& the green brown dunn of sudan of bel uur
of the great bent blow of the niger

crumbles into these flickering miles. the
silences of these hot holes of hell

drilled by the noon through the skull
into the bell of our belly

marrow burning its protein to gravel
skin mouldered to ash

holocaust of dome
souls propped up on sticks of skeletones

ball headed children
naked of all else but their large deep agate space age eyes

their crystal tears all gone gone dead gone white gone salt
gone silent

their blue skulls cracked like eggs with dirt with puss with
postule

who can no longer run or walk or even limp across these
spaces

whose wordless cries come from a dry rag mouth around a
thirsty

bone

my little halted lonely children of the desert
flies dying into crevices from all the fertile places

slack bladders of dried milk hang haggard from my
mannequin

with only memories of nipple suck suck. ing their blistered
lips

the film crews cameras already closing in
like buzz like buzzards on this moonscape manscape in slow

motion

herds.
men be.

come scare.
crows

their howls of silent dante lamentations wheeling across the
supersands like paper water in. to the shadow of this eye

this i/
cicle this eye.

less rise.
ing gas face mountain

Soweto

for Nelson & Winnie Mandela

Out of this roar of innumerable demons

hot cinema tarzan sweat
rolling moth ball eyes yellow teeth
cries of claws slashes clanks   *opposition*

a faint high pallor

dust

oceans rolling over the dry sand of the savanna

your houses homes warm still with the buffalo milk
bladder of elephant . tusk of his stripped tree
sing soft clinks

                          warmth: nature
but the barracks   *coolness: Soweto/city*

the dark dark barks of the shark
boys
the cool juice of soweto. . .

75

Soweto

images of destruction

■

out of this dust they are coming
our eyes listen out of rhinoceros thunder
darkness of lion

the whale roar stomping in heaven
that black bellied night of hell and helleluia
when all the lights of anger flicker flicker flicker flicker

and we know somewhere there there is <u>real fire</u>   *as opposed to the bullhorn kleghorn*
basuto mokhethi namibia azania shaka the zulu kenyatta the shatt
erer the maasai wandering into the everlasting shadow of jah

daughters lost daughters

bellowing against bullhorn and kleghorn
bellowing against bargwart and the searchlights of dogs   *reaction against white violence apartheid*
bellowing against crick and the kick in the stomach

the acrid wretch against the teeth
bellowing against <u>malan</u> malan malam malan
and boer and <u>boerwreck</u> and <u>boertrek</u> and truckloads of metal

helmet and fusil and the <u>hand</u> grenade
and acid <u>rhodes</u> and the diamonds of <u>oppenheimer</u>
the opulence of voortresshers the grass streiders. . .

*white power
the city is a white creation*

76

suddenly like that fire the crows in johannesburg
you were there
torn. in tears. tatters   *you: Soweto?*
                            horrid place to live in
but the eyes glittered and the fist   *a ghetto'.*
clenching around that scream of your mother bled   *& yet*
into a black head of hammers

and the night fell howl ~ *poetic sig. of howl*
on soweto

the night fell howl
on soweto

and we who had failed to listen all. those. foot. steps -
who had given you up like a torn paper package

your heroes   burning in your houses
                   rising from your dust bowls
                   flaring from the sky

                   listen now as the news items lengthen
                   gathering like hawks looking upward like the
                   leopard plunging into the turmoil like the

                   constrictor

and that crouch/shot
shout out against that beast and pistol
the police who shot patrice who castrated kimathi
        reaction against whitey

and clattering clattering clattering clattering
the veldts gun metals wings
rise from their last supper their hunger of bones

bomba

and the daniels sing *personification of justice*

ukufa akuqheleki kodwa ke
kuthiwa akuhlanga lungehlanga
lalani ngenxeba nikhuzeka

and we are rowing out to sea where the woman
lived with her pipe and her smoke
shack

and her tea in the tea
pot
tankard of hopes

herbs

lamagora afele
izwe lawo

and we are rowing out to sea
where there are farms

and our farmers laid waste the land
to make honey. we are the bells of the land. . .

dumminit
dumminit

lit by lantern and lamp

damp
dumminit

ash/can
kero

sene glow
can

dle &
glare

dumminit

hitting the head of the h/anvil

huh

drumminit

■

his school/book
huh

but to learn
blood

what is blood
hah

                                                but to bless
                                                dream

and that hill now under the ocean
and the pages splashed with his blood
and that bullet a hero a hero herero. . .

hero from Soweto uprising

■

once the germans destroyed every sperm
in your village every man who could walk
every nim growing into the noom and nam of yr man/hood

*showing that
the history
of colonization
is that
of*

they stripped skin and made catapults skulls were their pelmets
upon the wall
and the torn feet cracked and stacked and streggaed

rubbish heap . dog howl . cenotaph

*fatal noon
rhymes w/ doom*

and for days there was stench over the grasslands
and for months there was silence upon the trees
cow . goat . udder . manyatta

*uprooting
→
oppression.*

bantustan upon the land. . .

and then it was gone like all hero hero herero
like your canoe upon the land. . .

80

■

walking back down now from the shores of kikuyu water
washing back down now from swahili laughter

zimbabwe kinshasa limpopo
always limpopo the limper the healer

it comes down from the ruins of the north
from the lakes of the luo

from the sunlights and sunrise of the east

as antient as sheba as wise as the pharaohs
as holy as the early morning mists of ityopia

an i
man
tek long
time to
reach hey
but a
bomb
an de lim
popo drop
down
an de
dread
come
an de
wreck
age soon
done

soon

soon

soweto

we have waited so long for this signal
     this howl of your silence
     this heat of herero this hero

and i beheld the great beast strangled
     howling in its chains
     led by the fetlocks
     and the opulence useless
and the long guns shattered and silent

.

and we rise

mushroom

cloud

mau mau

kilimanjaro

silvers of eagles

tears

savannas

nzingas of rivers

waiting for
~ some sign of revolt
from
Soweto

82

umklaklabulus of mountains

and the unutterable metal of the

volcano

serves as metaphor for revolt

rising

rising

rising

burning

soon

soon

soon

soweto

bongo man a come
bongo man a come

bruggadung

bongo man a come
bongo man a come

bruggadung
bruggadung

bruggadung
bruggadung

break it down
imperative to wipe out
oppression

Leopard

forever Doföe

read!
midterm!

The Leopard has been
   caught & caged much
    as the African people
        were caught & caged: metaphorically by the colonizers

Caught therefore in this care-
ful cage of glint. rock

water ringing the islands'
doubt. his

terror dares
not blink. a nerv-

ous tick-like
itch

picks
at the corners of his

lips. the lean flanks quick
& quiv-

er until the ten-
sion cracks his

ribs. if he could only
strike or

trigger off
his fury. but cunning

cold bars break his
rage &

stretched to strike
his stretched claws strike no glory

2

There was a land not long   *A frica*
ago where it was other-
wise. where he was happy

that fatal plunge down from the
tree on antelope or duiker
was freedom for him then

But somewhere in the dampened
dark the marks-
man watched. the strings were   *Colonizer/slave-trader*

stretched. the tricky traps were
ready. Yet had he felt
his supple force would fall

to such confinement
would he. to dodge his doom
& guarantee his movemant

have paused from stalking deer   *brutal by human*
or striking down the duiker   *standards*
or would he. face to fate

have merely murdered more? *?*
                            .

3

But he must do
what fate had forced him to

88

at birth his blood
was bent upon a flood

that forged him forward
on its deadly springes

his paws grew heavy
and his claws shone sharp

unleashed. his passion
slashed & mangled with its stain-

less steel
no flesh he raped

would ever
heal. like grape

crushed in the mouth to you
was each new death

to him
each death he dealt perfected him   as ~~OKPO~~
                                      Okonkwo felt ~~death~~ his
his victims felt this single   killings in war perfected
soft intention in him. as gentle   him.

as a pigeon . winging home

4

Now he stands caged
the monkeys lisp & leer

and rip & hammer
at the barriers

he burns & paces
turns again & paces
disdaining admiration in those faces
that peer & pander at him through the barriers

Give him a tree to leap from
liberator
in pity let him once more move
with his soft spotted & untroubled splendour

among the thrills & whispers of his glint-
ing king-
dom. or unlock him
and now let him from his trigger-

ed branch
& guillotining vantage
in one fine _final_ fall-
ing fall upon the quick fear-

footed deer or peer-
less antelope _whose beauty_
ravaged with his brutal sharp intention
propitiates the ancient guilt
appeases   *very sig.*
each feels toward the other
the victim's wish to hurt — *strike back*
the hunter's not to   *The African's wish*
and by this scarifice   *to strike back*

of strong to helpless other
healed & aneled *annointed*

90

both hurt & hunter
by this fatal lunge made whole

Letter
Sycorax

forest Nzinga

1

Dear mamma

*i writin yu dis letter/**wha?***
guess what! pun a computer o/kay?
like i jine de mercantilists!

well not quite!

i mean de same way dem tief/in gun
power from sheena & taken we blues &

gone

■ ■ ■

say
wha? get on wid de same ole

story?

okay
okay
okay
okay

if yu cyaan beat prospero
whistle

No mamma!

is not one a dem pensive tings like ibm or
bang & ovid
nor anyting glori. ous like dat!

but is one a de bess tings since cicero o
kay?

it have key
board &

evva

ting. like dat ole
reminton yu have pun top de war. drobe up
there ketchin duss

only wid dis one yu na ave to benn dung over
to out out
de mistake dem wid white liquid paper. de
papyrus

ribbid & soff

before it drei up flakey &
crink. like yu was paintin yu house

um doan even nuse no paper yu does have to
roll
pun dat blk rollin pin like yu rollin dough pun
a flatten

& does go off ping pun de right hann wing a
de paper
when de clatterin words start to fly & fling
like a ping. wing

.

wid dis **X** *now*
long before yu cud say jackie robb
inson or rt-d2 or shout

wre **X**

dis ya obeah blo **X**
get a whole whole para
graph write up &

blink
pun a black
bird

like dat indonesian fella in star
trek
where dem is wear dem permanent wrinkle up
grey

& white flannel cost
ume like dem gettin ready to
jogg

but dem sittin dung dere in such silence a
rome

it not turn
in a hair pun dem wig/wam &

hack/in out hack/in hack/in all sorta back
up & read
out & fail

out & think &
it even have trash
can for garbage from all part/icles a de gal.
a *y*

&
mamma

a doan really know how pascal & co.
balt & apple & cogito ergo sum
come to h/invent all these tings since

de rice & fall a de roman empire
& how capitalism & slaveley like it putt
christianity
on ice

so dem cd always open dat cole
smokin door a hell when dem ready for ash or
a psalm
sangridge or

choke

Why i cyaan nuse me hann & crawl
up de white like i use
to?

since when i kin
type?

**dats wat i tryin to tell
ya!**

*yu know me cyaan
neither flat
foot pun de key*

*boards like
say
charlie chap dance/in*

*far
less touch
tapp/in like bo.*

jangles

*walk/in down chauncery
lane*

yu hear/in me mwa?

but i
mwangles!

■

a mean
a nat farwardin wid star
wars

nor sing
songin no bionicle
songs or like sputnik &

chips
goin bleep bleep bleep bleep bleep bleep bleep
into de peloponnesian wars

but i
mwangles

2

Why a callin it

𝑋?

a doan write.
ly know
but yes.
taday when a was tell.

in a ceratin girl
frenn about

it/she kinda look at i funn.
y like if

she tink i has 𝑋er𝑋es or aids

so she soffly soffly silk.
in i off like if i is sick.

ly or sorrow or
souse

but is like what i try.
in to sen/seh &

seh about muse.
in computer

& mouse &
learn.

in prospero ling.
go

&
ting

not fe dem/not fe dem
de way caliban

done

but fe we
fe a-we

for nat one a we shd response if prospero get
curse
wid im own
curser

though um not like when covetous ride miss
praedial
mule

but is like we still start
where we start/in out start/in out start/in
out start/in

out
since menelek was a bwoy
& why is dat &

what is de bess way to say so/so it doan sounn
like

brigg
flatts or her. vokitz nor de

π.
san cantos nor de souf sea bible

nor like ink. le & yarico & de anglo saxon
chronicles

&
mamma!

a fine
a cyaan get nutten

write
a cyaan get nutten really

rite
while a stannin up hey in me years & like me
inside a me shadow

like de mahn still mekkin mwe walk up de
slope dat e slide
in black down de whole long curve a de arch

i

pell

a

go

some
times smile.
in nice

some
times like e   really laughin   after we &
some
times like e   helpin we up   while e push.

in we black dung
again

like when yu rumbellin
dung
into de under

grounn

on one a dem move.
in stair
crace &

like yu fuh.
get like yu wallet or some
ting like

dat
& yu cyaan nevva turn
back

nor
walk back up
nor

even run back
up

outta there

■

cause de stair.
crace
crazy &

creak.
in & snake
skinn. in

it

down
down
down

&

how. ever
yu
runnin up runnin up runnin up runnin up

it still

goin down
goin down
goin down
goin down

like sa.
hell

like sy.
phyllis

like
the edges of the desert

&

guess who down dey at de top
a de line wid dante & dodo & julie &

nappo & nix & adolph
kaisermann be. havin like one a de boys

but idi & splash & pol
pot

&
a whole rash a economists pullin we up by we
boot

straps & smo. kin
pot
bellied ha/ha/ha/ha/havana cigars

& grand master sergeant doe &
brand new imperial corporals smilin of

cordite &
leather

strap & vd & vid.
eo

&

the
striped eyes of nigerian tigritude
& like what yu say happ.

enin inna
libraria

all a dem brooks of the dead
&

mamma

a know yu can plant lettice & nice but yu
cyaaann eat ikebana

Yet a sittin dung here in front a dis stone
face

eeee
lectrical mallet into me

fist

chipp/in dis poem onta dis tab.
let

chiss. ellin dark.
ness writin in light

like i is a some. is a some. is a some
body.

a X
pert or some

thing like moses or aaron or one a dem
dyaaam isra
light

&
mamma!

Irae

for Jere

Dies irae dreadful day
when the world shall pass away
so the priests & showmen say

what gaunt phantoms shall affront me
my lai sharpville wounded knee
arthur kissorcallatme

to what judgement meekly led
shall men gather trumpeted
by louis armstrong from the dead

life & death shall here be voice
less rising from their moist
interment hoist

ing all their flags before them
poniard poison rocket bomb
nations of the earth shall come

& his record page on page
forever building he shall scan & give each age
sentences of righteous rage

if the pious then shall shake me
what reply can merchants make me
what defences can they fake?

mighty & majestic god
head saviour of the broken herd
heal me nanny cuffee cudjoe
grant me mercy give me sword

day of fire dreadful day
day for which all sufferers pray
grant me patience with thy plenty
grant me vengeance with thy word